Mastering Solidity: A Comprehensive Guide to Smart Contract Development

By Anthony Colasante

Table of Contents

- Gas Optimization Techniques
- Inline Assembly
- Proxy Contracts and Upgrades

1. **Smart Contract Security**
   - Common Vulnerabilities and Attack Vectors
   - Best Practices for Secure Coding
   - Auditing and Testing Your Contracts

1. **Introduction to Hardhat**
   - Overview and Installation
   - Setting Up a Hardhat Project
   - Compiling and Deploying Contracts
   - Writing and Running Tests

1. **Advanced Hardhat Techniques**
   - Debugging with Hardhat
   - Using Hardhat Plugins
   - Integrating with Frontend Applications
   - Deploying to Different Networks

1. **Introduction to Foundry**
   - Overview and Installation
   - Setting Up a Foundry Project
   -

Chapter 1: Introduction to Solidity Programming

Overview of Blockchain and Smart Contracts

What is Blockchain?

Blockchain is a decentralized, distributed ledger technology that securely records transactions across many computers. This decentralized nature ensures that data cannot be altered retroactively without altering all subsequent blocks, making blockchain highly secure and transparent. Here are some key features of blockchain:

- **Decentralization:** No single entity controls the blockchain; it is maintained by a network of nodes.
- **Transparency:** All transactions are recorded on a public ledger that is accessible to everyone.
- **Immutability:** Once data is recorded on the blockchain, it cannot be changed or deleted.
- **Security:** Cryptographic algorithms secure transactions and data on the blockchain.

What are Smart Contracts?

Smart contracts are self-executing contracts with the terms of the agreement directly written into code. They run on the blockchain, ensuring that they are transparent, immutable, and decentralized. Smart contracts automate and enforce agreements, reducing the need for intermediaries and increasing efficiency. Key characteristics of smart contracts include:

- **Automation:** Smart contracts automatically execute actions when predefined conditions are met.
- **Trustlessness:** Parties can trust the code without needing to trust each other.
- **Efficiency:** Automated processes reduce the time and cost associated with traditional contracts.
-

  Transparency: All contract terms and execution details are visible and verifiable on the blockchain.

Introduction to Solidity

What is Solidity?

Solidity is a statically-typed programming language designed for developing smart contracts that run on the Ethereum Virtual Machine (EVM). It is influenced by JavaScript, Python, and C++, making it relatively easy for developers familiar with these languages to learn. Solidity enables developers to write smart contracts that can manage and enforce the rules of complex applications, such as decentralized finance (DeFi) protocols, voting systems, and more.

Why Learn Solidity?

- **Growing Demand:** The popularity of blockchain technology and decentralized applications (dApps) is increasing, creating a demand for skilled Solidity developers.

- **Versatility:** Solidity is used to develop a wide range of applications, from simple token contracts to complex decentralized exchanges (DEXs).

- **Community and Resources:** A large and active community provides extensive resources, libraries, and tools to support Solidity development.

- **Career Opportunities:** Proficiency in Solidity opens up numerous career opportunities in the blockchain space, including development, auditing, and consulting roles.

Setting Up Your Development Environment

Prerequisites

Before diving into Solidity programming, ensure you have the following prerequisites:

- **Basic Programming Knowledge:** Familiarity with basic programming concepts (variables, functions, loops) is helpful.

- **Node.js and npm:** Node.js and npm (Node Package Manager) are required to install and manage development tools. You can download them from the official Node.js website.

Installing Node.js and npm

1. **Download and Install:** Visit the Node.js website and download the LTS (Long-Term Support) version. Follow the installation instructions for your operating system.

Verify Installation: Open a terminal or command prompt and run the following commands to verify the installation:
bash
Copy code
node -v
npm -v

    1.

Installing Hardhat

Hardhat is a development environment for compiling, deploying, testing, and debugging Ethereum smart contracts. It provides a flexible and extensible framework to streamline Solidity development.

Create a Project Directory:
bash
Copy code
mkdir my-solidity-project
cd my-solidity-project

    1.

Initialize a New Node.js Project:
bash
Copy code
npm init -y

    1.

Install Hardhat:
bash

Copy code
```
npm install --save-dev hardhat
```

    1.

Create a Hardhat Project:
bash
Copy code
```
npx hardhat
```

    1. Follow the prompts to create a new Hardhat project. Choose the default options for a basic setup.

Installing Foundry

Foundry is another powerful tool for Solidity development, offering a different set of features and benefits compared to Hardhat.

    1. **Install Foundry:** Follow the instructions on the Foundry GitHub repository to install Foundry.

Initialize a Foundry Project:
bash
Copy code
```
forge init my-foundry-project
cd my-foundry-project
```

    1.

Setting Up Your Code Editor

Using a code editor with Solidity support can significantly enhance your development experience. Popular options include:

-

Visual Studio Code (VS Code): A widely-used code editor with excellent Solidity support through extensions like "Solidity" by Juan Blanco.

●

Remix IDE: An online Integrated Development Environment specifically designed for Solidity development.

Configuring VS Code for Solidity

1. **Install VS Code:** Download and install VS Code from the official website.
2. **Install Solidity Extension:** Open VS Code, go to the Extensions view (Ctrl+Shift+X), and search for "Solidity." Install the extension by Juan Blanco.
3. **Optional Extensions:** Consider installing additional extensions for linting, formatting, and debugging, such as "Prettier - Code formatter" and "Solidity Visual Developer."

Summary

In this chapter, we introduced the fundamental concepts of blockchain and smart contracts, emphasizing their significance in modern technology. We also provided an overview of Solidity, the primary language for developing Ethereum smart contracts, and guided you through setting up your development environment with tools like Hardhat and Foundry.

With your environment ready, you're now prepared to dive into Solidity basics and start writing your first smart contracts. In the next chapter, we will explore Solidity data types, variables, functions, and conditionals, laying the groundwork for your journey into smart contract development.

Chapter 2: Solidity Basics

Data Types and Variables

Basic Data Types

Solidity provides a variety of basic data types that are used to declare variables. Understanding these data types is crucial for writing efficient and effective smart contracts.

Boolean: Represents true or false values.
solidity
Copy code
```
bool isActive = true;
```
  •

Integer: Represents both signed (int) and unsigned (uint) integers.
solidity
Copy code
```
int256 balance = -100;
uint256 amount = 100;
```
  •

Address: Holds a 20-byte Ethereum address.
solidity
Copy code
```
address owner =
0x1234567890123456789012345678901234567890;
```
  •

Bytes: Represents a fixed-size byte array.
solidity
Copy code
```
bytes32 data = "Hello, World!";
```

-

String: Represents a dynamically-sized UTF-8 encoded string.
solidity
Copy code
```solidity
string message = "Hello, Blockchain!";
```
-

Declaring Variables

Variables in Solidity can be declared using specific data types, followed by the variable name and an optional initial value.

solidity
Copy code
```solidity
uint256 public totalSupply = 1000000;
address public contractOwner = msg.sender;
bool public isAvailable = true;
```

Constants and Immutable Variables

Constants: Variables that cannot be changed once assigned.
solidity
Copy code
```solidity
uint256 public constant MAX_SUPPLY = 1000000;
```
-

Immutable: Variables that can be assigned only once, typically during contract deployment.
solidity
Copy code
```solidity
address public immutable OWNER;
constructor() {
    OWNER = msg.sender;
}
```
-

Functions and Conditionals

Functions

Functions are the building blocks of Solidity contracts, used to define the behavior and actions of the contract.

Function Declaration:
solidity
Copy code
```
function getBalance() public view returns (uint256) {
    return balance;
}
```

-
-

   Function Modifiers:
   - **public:** Accessible from anywhere.
   - **private:** Accessible only within the contract.
   - **internal:** Accessible within the contract and derived contracts.
   - **external:** Accessible only from external calls.

-
   Function Types:
   - **view:** Indicates that the function does not alter the state.

   - **pure:** Indicates that the function does not read or alter the state.

Conditionals

Solidity supports traditional control flow statements like if-else.

If-Else Statement:
solidity
Copy code
```
function checkBalance(uint256 amount) public view returns (bool)
{
   if (balance >= amount) {
      return true;
   } else {
      return false;
   }
}
```
   •

Arrays and Structs

Arrays

Arrays are used to store multiple values of the same type.

Fixed-size Array:
solidity
Copy code
```
uint[5] public fixedArray = [1, 2, 3, 4, 5];
```
   •

Dynamic Array:
solidity
Copy code
```
uint[] public dynamicArray;
function addElement(uint element) public {
   dynamicArray.push(element);
}
```
   •

Structs

Structs allow you to create custom data types that group together related data.

solidity
Copy code

```solidity
struct User {
   uint id;
   string name;
   address wallet;
}
User[] public users;
function addUser(uint _id, string memory _name, address _wallet) public {
   users.push(User(_id, _name, _wallet));
}
```

Mappings and Enums

Mappings

Mappings are used to store key-value pairs.

solidity
Copy code

```solidity
mapping(address => uint) public balances;
function updateBalance(address _user, uint _balance) public {
   balances[_user] = _balance;
}
function getBalance(address _user) public view returns (uint) {
   return balances[_user];
}
```

Enums

Enums are used to create user-defined types with a finite set of constant values.

solidity
Copy code
```solidity
enum Status { Active, Inactive, Suspended }
Status public currentStatus;
function setStatus(Status _status) public {
    currentStatus = _status;
}
function getStatus() public view returns (Status) {
    return currentStatus;
}
```

Control Structures and Loops

If-Else Statements

The if-else statement is used to execute code based on certain conditions.

solidity
Copy code
```solidity
function checkEligibility(uint age) public pure returns (string memory) {
    if (age >= 18) {
        return "Eligible";
    } else {
        return "Not Eligible";
    }
}
```

For and While Loops

Loops are used to repeatedly execute a block of code.

For Loop:
solidity
Copy code
```solidity
function sum(uint n) public pure returns (uint) {
```

```solidity
    uint total = 0;
    for (uint i = 0; i <= n; i++) {
        total += i;
    }
    return total;
}
```

-

While Loop:
solidity
Copy code
```solidity
function factorial(uint n) public pure returns (uint) {
    uint result = 1;
    uint i = n;
    while (i > 0) {
        result *= i;
        i--;
    }
    return result;
}
```

-

Break and Continue

The break statement exits the loop, while continue skips to the next iteration.

Break:
solidity
Copy code
```solidity
function findNumber(uint[] memory numbers, uint target) public
pure returns (bool) {
    for (uint i = 0; i < numbers.length; i++) {
        if (numbers[i] == target) {
            return true;
        }
    }
}
```

```solidity
    return false;
}
```

-

Continue:
solidity
Copy code
```solidity
function skipEvenNumbers(uint n) public pure returns (uint[]
memory) {
    uint[] memory result = new uint[](n/2);
    uint counter = 0;
    for (uint i = 0; i < n; i++) {
        if (i % 2 == 0) {
            continue;
        }
        result[counter] = i;
        counter++;
    }
    return result;
}
```

-

Summary

In this chapter, we covered the foundational elements of Solidity, including data types, variables, functions, conditionals, arrays, structs, mappings, enums, and control structures. Understanding these basics is essential for building more complex smart contracts. In the next chapter, we will delve into contract development, where you'll learn how to create, deploy, and manage your first Solidity contract.

Chapter 3: Contract Development

Creating and Deploying Your First Contract

Writing Your First Contract

Let's start by writing a simple Solidity contract. This contract will store and retrieve a number.

solidity

Copy code

```solidity
// SPDX-License-Identifier: MIT

pragma solidity ^0.8.0;

contract SimpleStorage {

    uint256 private storedNumber;

    function set(uint256 _number) public {

        storedNumber = _number;

    }

    function get() public view returns (uint256) {

        return storedNumber;

    }
```

}

Compiling the Contract

To compile your Solidity contract, you need to have a development environment set up. We'll use Hardhat for this example.

Install Hardhat (if not already installed):
bash
Copy code
npm install --save-dev hardhat

1.

Create a new Hardhat project:
bash
Copy code
npx hardhat

1. Follow the prompts to create a basic sample project.
2. **Place your contract in the contracts directory.**

Compile the contract:
bash
Copy code
npx hardhat compile

1.

Deploying the Contract

To deploy the contract, create a deployment script in the scripts directory.

Create a new file named deploy.js in the scripts directory:
javascript

Copy code
```
async function main() {

    const [deployer] = await ethers.getSigners();

    console.log("Deploying contracts with the account:",
deployer.address);

    const SimpleStorage = await
ethers.getContractFactory("SimpleStorage");

    const simpleStorage = await SimpleStorage.deploy();

    console.log("SimpleStorage deployed to:",
simpleStorage.address);

}

main()

  .then(() => process.exit(0))

  .catch(error => {

    console.error(error);

    process.exit(1);

  });
```

1.

Run the deployment script:
bash
Copy code
```
npx hardhat run scripts/deploy.js --network <network-name>
```

1. Replace <network-name> with your chosen
   network, such as localhost or ropsten.

Inheritance and Visibility

Inheritance

Inheritance allows you to create new contracts that are based on existing contracts. This helps in reusing code and creating hierarchical contract structures.

solidity

Copy code

```solidity
// SPDX-License-Identifier: MIT

pragma solidity ^0.8.0;

contract Parent {

    string public message;

    function setMessage(string memory _message) public {

        message = _message;

    }

}

contract Child is Parent {

    function getMessage() public view returns (string memory) {

        return message;

    }

}
```

Visibility

Visibility modifiers define who can access certain functions and variables. There are four visibility types in Solidity:

- **public:** Accessible from anywhere.

- **private:** Accessible only within the contract.

- **internal:** Accessible within the contract and derived contracts.

- **external:** Accessible only from external calls.

solidity

Copy code

```solidity
// SPDX-License-Identifier: MIT

pragma solidity ^0.8.0;

contract VisibilityExample {

    uint256 public publicVar = 1;

    uint256 private privateVar = 2;

    uint256 internal internalVar = 3;

    function publicFunction() public view returns (uint256) {

        return publicVar;

    }

    function privateFunction() private view returns (uint256) {

        return privateVar;
```

```
    }

    function internalFunction() internal view returns (uint256) {

        return internalVar;

    }

    function externalFunction() external view returns (uint256) {

        return publicVar;

    }

}
```

Function Modifiers

Function modifiers are used to modify the behavior of functions. They can be used to add pre-conditions or post-conditions to functions.

solidity

Copy code

```
// SPDX-License-Identifier: MIT

pragma solidity ^0.8.0;

contract ModifierExample {

    address public owner;

    uint256 public value;

    constructor() {

        owner = msg.sender;
```

```solidity
    }

    modifier onlyOwner() {

        require(msg.sender == owner, "Not the contract owner");

        _;

    }

    function setValue(uint256 _value) public onlyOwner {

        value = _value;

    }

}
```

Events and Logging

Events allow you to log data to the blockchain, which can be useful for off-chain applications.

solidity

Copy code

```solidity
// SPDX-License-Identifier: MIT

pragma solidity ^0.8.0;

contract EventExample {

    event ValueChanged(uint256 newValue);

    uint256 public value;

    function setValue(uint256 _value) public {
```

```
        value = _value;

        emit ValueChanged(_value);

    }

}
```

Listening to Events

You can listen to events in your frontend application using libraries like ethers.js or web3.js.

javascript

Copy code

```javascript
const contract = new ethers.Contract(contractAddress, contractABI, provider);

contract.on("ValueChanged", (newValue) => {

    console.log("Value changed to:", newValue.toString());

});
```

Summary

In this chapter, we covered the basics of contract development, including creating and deploying a simple contract, using inheritance and visibility modifiers, applying function modifiers, and logging events. These concepts form the foundation of developing more complex smart contracts. In the next chapter, we will explore advanced Solidity concepts such as error handling, gas optimization, inline assembly, proxy contracts, and upgrades.

Chapter 4: Advanced Solidity Concepts

Error Handling and Require

Error Handling

Error handling in Solidity is crucial for building robust and secure smart contracts. Solidity provides several ways to handle errors:

- **Require:** Ensures that certain conditions are met before executing the function.
- **Assert:** Used to check for conditions that should never occur.
- **Revert:** Reverts the transaction and provides an error message.

Require

The require statement is used to validate conditions and throw an error if the condition is not met. It is commonly used for input validation and access control.

solidity

Copy code

```
// SPDX-License-Identifier: MIT

pragma solidity ^0.8.0;
```

```solidity
contract RequireExample {

    address public owner;

    constructor() {

        owner = msg.sender;

    }

    function setValue(uint256 _value) public view returns (uint256)
{

        require(msg.sender == owner, "Caller is not the owner");

        require(_value > 0, "Value must be greater than zero");

        return _value;

    }

}
```

Assert

The assert statement is used to check for conditions that should never occur. If the condition is false, the transaction is reverted, and all gas is consumed.

solidity

Copy code

```solidity
// SPDX-License-Identifier: MIT

pragma solidity ^0.8.0;

contract AssertExample {

    uint256 public value;
```

```solidity
function setValue(uint256 _value) public {

    value = _value;

    assert(value == _value); // This should always be true

  }

}
```

Revert

The revert statement is used to revert the transaction and provide an error message. It is often used in complex functions where multiple conditions need to be checked.

solidity

Copy code

```solidity
// SPDX-License-Identifier: MIT

pragma solidity ^0.8.0;

contract RevertExample {

  address public owner;

  constructor() {

    owner = msg.sender;

  }

  function withdraw(uint256 amount) public {

    if (msg.sender != owner) {

      revert("Caller is not the owner");
```

```
        }

    if (amount > address(this).balance) {

        revert("Insufficient balance");

    }

    payable(owner).transfer(amount);

    }

}
```

Gas Optimization Techniques

Overview

Gas optimization is crucial for writing cost-effective smart contracts. Optimizing gas usage reduces transaction costs and improves the efficiency of smart contracts.

Common Techniques

Minimize Storage Writes: Writing to storage is more expensive than reading from storage. Minimize the number of storage writes in your contract.
solidity
Copy code

```solidity
// Inefficient

contract GasInefficient {

    uint256 public count;

    function increment() public {

        count = count + 1;
```

```
    }

}
```

// Efficient

```
contract GasEfficient {

    uint256 public count;

    function increment() public {

        uint256 newCount = count + 1;

        count = newCount;

    }

}
```

1.

Use calldata for Function Parameters: When possible, use calldata instead of memory for function parameters. Calldata is cheaper than memory.
solidity
Copy code
// More expensive

```
function processData(string memory data) public {

    // ...

}
```

// Less expensive

```
function processData(string calldata data) public {

    // ...
```

}

    1.

Avoid Dynamic Arrays in Storage: Dynamic arrays in storage are expensive to manage. Use fixed-size arrays or mappings when possible.
solidity
Copy code

```solidity
// Inefficient

uint256[] public dynamicArray;

// Efficient

uint256[10] public fixedArray;
```

    1.

Inline Assembly

Introduction

Inline assembly allows you to write low-level assembly code within your Solidity contract. It provides greater control over the EVM and can be used for gas optimization and other advanced use cases.

Example

Here is an example of using inline assembly to perform a simple arithmetic operation.

solidity

Copy code

```solidity
// SPDX-License-Identifier: MIT
```

```solidity
pragma solidity ^0.8.0;

contract AssemblyExample {

    function add(uint256 a, uint256 b) public pure returns (uint256 result) {

        assembly {

            result := add(a, b)

        }

    }

}
```

Proxy Contracts and Upgrades

Overview

Proxy contracts enable you to upgrade your smart contracts without changing their addresses. This is essential for maintaining contract state and ensuring continuity.

How It Works

1. **Proxy Contract:** Acts as an interface and delegates calls to the implementation contract.
2. **Implementation Contract:** Contains the actual logic and can be upgraded as needed.

Example

Here is a simplified example of a proxy contract:

solidity

Copy code

```solidity
// SPDX-License-Identifier: MIT

pragma solidity ^0.8.0;

contract Proxy {

  address public implementation;

  constructor(address _implementation) {

    implementation = _implementation;

  }

  fallback() external {

    (bool success, bytes memory data) =
implementation.delegatecall(msg.data);

    require(success, "Delegatecall failed");

  }

  function upgrade(address _newImplementation) public {

    implementation = _newImplementation;

  }

}
```

Summary

In this chapter, we explored advanced Solidity concepts, including
error handling with require, assert, and revert, gas optimization
techniques, inline assembly for low-level operations, and proxy
contracts for upgradability. Mastering these concepts will help you

write more efficient, secure, and maintainable smart contracts. In the next chapter, we will delve into smart contract security, covering common vulnerabilities, best practices for secure coding, and methods for auditing and testing your contracts.

Chapter 5: Smart Contract Security

Common Vulnerabilities and Attack Vectors

Reentrancy Attacks

A reentrancy attack occurs when a malicious contract repeatedly calls a function before the previous function call is completed. This can drain funds from a contract.

Example:

solidity

Copy code

```solidity
// SPDX-License-Identifier: MIT

pragma solidity ^0.8.0;

contract VulnerableContract {

    mapping(address => uint256) public balances;

    function deposit() public payable {

        balances[msg.sender] += msg.value;

    }

    function withdraw(uint256 _amount) public {
```

```solidity
    require(balances[msg.sender] >= _amount, "Insufficient
balance");

    (bool success, ) = msg.sender.call{value: _amount}("");

    require(success, "Transfer failed");

    balances[msg.sender] -= _amount;

    }

}
```

Mitigation:

Use the Checks-Effects-Interactions Pattern:
solidity
Copy code
```solidity
function withdraw(uint256 _amount) public {

    require(balances[msg.sender] >= _amount, "Insufficient
balance");

    balances[msg.sender] -= _amount;

    (bool success, ) = msg.sender.call{value: _amount}("");

    require(success, "Transfer failed");

}
```

1.

Use Reentrancy Guards:
solidity
Copy code
```solidity
import "@openzeppelin/contracts/security/ReentrancyGuard.sol";

contract SecureContract is ReentrancyGuard {
```

```solidity
function withdraw(uint256 _amount) public nonReentrant {

    require(balances[msg.sender] >= _amount, "Insufficient balance");

    balances[msg.sender] -= _amount;

    (bool success, ) = msg.sender.call{value: _amount}("");

    require(success, "Transfer failed");

  }

}
```

1.

Integer Overflow and Underflow

Integer overflow and underflow occur when arithmetic operations exceed the fixed size of the integer type, leading to unexpected results.

Example:

solidity

Copy code

```solidity
// SPDX-License-Identifier: MIT

pragma solidity ^0.8.0;

contract OverflowExample {

    function add(uint256 a, uint256 b) public pure returns (uint256)
{

        return a + b;
```

```
    }

}
```

Mitigation:

Use SafeMath Library:
solidity
Copy code
import "@openzeppelin/contracts/utils/math/SafeMath.sol";

contract SafeMathExample {

    using SafeMath for uint256;

    function add(uint256 a, uint256 b) public pure returns (uint256)
{

        return a.add(b);

    }

}

   1.

Front-Running Attacks

Front-running attacks occur when a malicious actor observes pending transactions and submits a similar transaction with higher gas fees to get it mined first.

Example:

solidity

Copy code

// SPDX-License-Identifier: MIT

```solidity
pragma solidity ^0.8.0;

contract Auction {

    uint256 public highestBid;

    function bid() public payable {

        require(msg.value > highestBid, "Bid too low");

        highestBid = msg.value;

    }

}
```

Mitigation:

Use Commit-Reveal Scheme:
solidity
Copy code
```solidity
contract SecureAuction {

    mapping(address => uint256) public bids;

    function commitBid(bytes32 _hashedBid) public {

        // Store hashed bid

    }

    function revealBid(uint256 _bid, bytes32 _salt) public {

        // Verify and update bid

    }

}
```

1.

Best Practices for Secure Coding

Use Established Libraries

Use well-established libraries like OpenZeppelin to avoid common pitfalls and vulnerabilities.

Follow the Principle of Least Privilege

Limit permissions and access rights to the minimum necessary to reduce the attack surface.

Regularly Audit and Test Contracts

Conduct regular audits and tests to identify and fix vulnerabilities. Use tools like MythX, Slither, and Echidna.

Keep Up with Security Updates

Stay informed about the latest security practices and updates in the Solidity and Ethereum communities.

Auditing and Testing Your Contracts

Auditing

Auditing involves a thorough review of your smart contract code to identify potential vulnerabilities.

1. **Manual Review:**
   - Check for common vulnerabilities.
   - Review code logic and flow.
   - Verify compliance with best practices.

1. **Automated Tools:**
    -

    MythX: A security analysis service for Ethereum smart contracts.
    -

    Slither: A static analysis tool to find vulnerabilities.
    -

    Echidna: A property-based testing tool for Ethereum.

Testing

Testing ensures that your contract functions as expected and handles edge cases.

1. **Unit Tests:**
    -

    Test individual functions and components.
    -

    Use frameworks like Hardhat and Truffle.

```javascript
Copy code
const { expect } = require("chai");

describe("SimpleStorage", function () {

  it("Should return the correct value", async function () {

    const SimpleStorage = await ethers.getContractFactory("SimpleStorage");

    const simpleStorage = await SimpleStorage.deploy();

    await simpleStorage.set(42);
```

```
    expect(await simpleStorage.get()).to.equal(42);

  });

});
```

1.
2. **Integration Tests:**
   ○

   Test interactions between multiple contracts and
   components.
1. **Property-Based Testing:**
   ○

   Use tools like Echidna to generate random test
   cases based on specified properties.

Best Practices for Testing

- **Test Coverage:** Ensure comprehensive test coverage for
  all functions and scenarios.
- **Mock External Dependencies:** Use mocks to simulate
  external dependencies and environments.
- **Continuous Integration (CI):** Integrate testing into your
  CI pipeline for automated and continuous testing.

Summary

In this chapter, we delved into smart contract security, exploring
common vulnerabilities such as reentrancy, integer overflow, and
front-running attacks, and their mitigations. We also covered best
practices for secure coding, including using established libraries,
following the principle of least privilege, and conducting regular
audits and tests. By adhering to these practices and continuously

testing your contracts, you can build robust and secure smart contracts. In the next chapter, we will introduce Hardhat, a powerful development environment for Ethereum, and guide you through setting up a Hardhat project, compiling and deploying contracts, and writing and running tests.

Chapter 6: Introduction to Hardhat

Overview and Installation

What is Hardhat?

Hardhat is a comprehensive development environment for Ethereum that facilitates tasks such as compiling, deploying, testing, and debugging smart contracts. It provides a flexible and extensible framework that integrates smoothly with various tools and plugins.

Key Features of Hardhat

- **Task Runner:** Automate common tasks like compiling and deploying contracts.

- **Built-in Network:** A local Ethereum network for quick and easy testing.

- **Console:** An interactive JavaScript console for executing commands.

- **Plugins:** Extend Hardhat's functionality with a wide range of plugins.

Installing Hardhat

To install Hardhat, you need to have Node.js and npm installed on your system. Follow these steps to install Hardhat:

Create a New Project Directory:
bash
Copy code
mkdir my-hardhat-project

cd my-hardhat-project

     1.

Initialize a New Node.js Project:
bash
Copy code
npm init -y

     1.

Install Hardhat:
bash
Copy code
npm install --save-dev hardhat

     1.

Create a Hardhat Project:
bash
Copy code
npx hardhat

     1. Follow the prompts to create a basic sample project. This will set up the necessary files and directories.

Setting Up a Hardhat Project

Project Structure

After setting up your Hardhat project, you will have the following structure:

lua

Copy code

```
my-hardhat-project/
├── contracts/
│   └── Greeter.sol
├── scripts/
│   └── sample-script.js
├── test/
│   └── sample-test.js
├── hardhat.config.js
├── package.json
└── node_modules/
```

- **contracts/:** Contains Solidity contract files.
- **scripts/:** Contains deployment scripts.
- **test/:** Contains test scripts.
- **hardhat.config.js:** Hardhat configuration file.

Configuring Hardhat

The hardhat.config.js file is the central configuration file for your Hardhat project. Here you can define network settings, compiler options, and plugin configurations.

javascript

Copy code

```javascript
require("@nomiclabs/hardhat-waffle");

module.exports = {

  solidity: "0.8.0",

  networks: {

    hardhat: {},

    ropsten: {

      url:
"https://ropsten.infura.io/v3/YOUR_INFURA_PROJECT_ID",

      accounts: ["YOUR_PRIVATE_KEY"]

    }

  }

};
```

Compiling and Deploying Contracts

Compiling Contracts

To compile your Solidity contracts, run the following command:

bash

Copy code

```bash
npx hardhat compile
```

This will compile all the contracts in the contracts/ directory and generate the necessary artifacts in the artifacts/ directory.

Writing a Deployment Script

Create a deployment script in the scripts/ directory to deploy your contract.

Create a new file named deploy.js in the scripts/ directory:
javascript
Copy code

```javascript
async function main() {

  const [deployer] = await ethers.getSigners();

  console.log("Deploying contracts with the account:",
deployer.address);

  const Greeter = await ethers.getContractFactory("Greeter");

  const greeter = await Greeter.deploy("Hello, Hardhat!");

  console.log("Greeter deployed to:", greeter.address);

}

main()

  .then(() => process.exit(0))

  .catch((error) => {

    console.error(error);

    process.exit(1);

  });
```

1.

50

Run the deployment script:
bash
Copy code
```
npx hardhat run scripts/deploy.js --network <network-name>
```

1. Replace <network-name> with your chosen
   network, such as localhost or ropsten.

Writing and Running Tests

Writing Tests

Create test scripts in the test/ directory to test your contracts.

Create a new file named greeter-test.js in the test/ directory:
javascript
Copy code
```
const { expect } = require("chai");

describe("Greeter", function () {

  it("Should return the new greeting once it's changed", async
function () {

    const Greeter = await ethers.getContractFactory("Greeter");

    const greeter = await Greeter.deploy("Hello, world!");

    await greeter.deployed();

    expect(await greeter.greet()).to.equal("Hello, world!");

    const setGreetingTx = await greeter.setGreeting("Hola,
mundo!");

    // wait until the transaction is mined

    await setGreetingTx.wait();
```

```
expect(await greeter.greet()).to.equal("Hola, mundo!");

});

});
```

1.

Running Tests

To run your tests, use the following command:

bash

Copy code

```
npx hardhat test
```

This will execute all the test scripts in the test/ directory and display the results.

Summary

In this chapter, we introduced Hardhat, a powerful development environment for Ethereum. We covered the installation process, project setup, and the basic structure of a Hardhat project. We also demonstrated how to compile and deploy contracts, and how to write and run tests using Hardhat. With these foundational skills, you're well-equipped to develop, test, and deploy Solidity contracts efficiently. In the next chapter, we will explore advanced Hardhat techniques, including debugging, using plugins, integrating with frontend applications, and deploying to different networks.

Chapter 7: Advanced Hardhat Techniques

Debugging with Hardhat

Overview

Debugging smart contracts can be challenging due to the complexities of blockchain environments. Hardhat provides several tools and plugins to make this process easier, enabling you to identify and resolve issues effectively.

Using Hardhat Console

The Hardhat console is an interactive JavaScript console that allows you to interact with your smart contracts. You can use it to test functions, inspect contract states, and debug issues in real-time.

bash

Copy code

```
npx hardhat console
```

In the console, you can deploy contracts and call functions:

javascript

Copy code

```
const Greeter = await ethers.getContractFactory("Greeter");

const greeter = await Greeter.deploy("Hello, Hardhat!");
```

```
await greeter.deployed();
```

```
console.log(await greeter.greet()); // Output: Hello, Hardhat!
```

Hardhat Debugger

Hardhat Debugger is a powerful tool for debugging failed transactions. It provides detailed information about the state and events leading up to the failure.

bash

Copy code

```
npx hardhat node
```

Deploy your contract on the local Hardhat network, then run the debugger:

bash

Copy code

```
npx hardhat run scripts/deploy.js --network localhost
```

```
npx hardhat debug <tx-hash>
```

Using Console.log

Hardhat allows you to use console.log in your Solidity code for debugging purposes, similar to JavaScript.

Install Hardhat Console:
bash
Copy code
```
npm install --save-dev hardhat-truffle5-plugin
```

1.

Use console.log in your contract:
solidity
Copy code

```solidity
// SPDX-License-Identifier: MIT

pragma solidity ^0.8.0;

contract Greeter {

    string public greeting;

    constructor(string memory _greeting) {

        console.log("Deploying a Greeter with greeting:", _greeting);

        greeting = _greeting;

    }

    function greet() public view returns (string memory) {

        console.log("Greeting:", greeting);

        return greeting;

    }

    function setGreeting(string memory _greeting) public {

        console.log("Changing greeting from '%s' to '%s'", greeting, _greeting);

        greeting = _greeting;

    }

}
```

1.

Run your scripts:
bash
Copy code
npx hardhat run scripts/deploy.js --network localhost

     1.

Using Hardhat Plugins

Overview

Hardhat plugins extend the functionality of Hardhat, adding features like contract verification, gas reporting, and integration with other tools. Below are some popular plugins and how to use them.

Hardhat Ethers

The Hardhat Ethers plugin integrates ethers.js into Hardhat, providing a simple and efficient way to interact with Ethereum.

Install the plugin:
bash
Copy code
npm install --save-dev @nomiclabs/hardhat-ethers ethers

     1.

Configure Hardhat:
Add the plugin to hardhat.config.js:
javascript
Copy code

```javascript
require("@nomiclabs/hardhat-ethers");

module.exports = {

  solidity: "0.8.0",
```

```
};
```

1.

Hardhat Waffle

Hardhat Waffle integrates the Waffle testing framework into Hardhat, providing enhanced testing capabilities.

Install the plugin:
bash
Copy code
```
npm install --save-dev @nomiclabs/hardhat-waffle ethereum-waffle chai
```

1.

Configure Hardhat:
Add the plugin to hardhat.config.js:
javascript
Copy code
```
require("@nomiclabs/hardhat-waffle");

module.exports = {

  solidity: "0.8.0",

};
```

1.

Hardhat Gas Reporter

The Hardhat Gas Reporter plugin generates gas usage reports for your smart contract functions, helping you optimize gas consumption.

Install the plugin:
bash

Copy code
```
npm install --save-dev hardhat-gas-reporter
```

       1.

Configure Hardhat:
Add the plugin to hardhat.config.js:
javascript
Copy code
```
require("hardhat-gas-reporter");

module.exports = {

  solidity: "0.8.0",

  gasReporter: {

    enabled: true,

    currency: 'USD',

  }

};
```

       1.

Integrating with Frontend Applications

Overview

Integrating smart contracts with frontend applications allows users to interact with the blockchain through a user-friendly interface. We will use React and ethers.js for this purpose.

Setting Up a React Project

Create a new React project:
bash
Copy code
npx create-react-app my-dapp

cd my-dapp

       1.

Install ethers.js:
bash
Copy code
npm install ethers

       1.

Connecting to Your Contract

Create a contract directory inside src/ and copy the contract ABI and address:
javascript
Copy code

```
// src/contract/Greeter.json

{

  "address": "YOUR_CONTRACT_ADDRESS",

  "abi": [

    // Your contract ABI

  ]

}
```

       1.

Connect to the contract in your React app:

javascript
Copy code

```javascript
// src/App.js

import React, { useEffect, useState } from 'react';

import { ethers } from 'ethers';

import Greeter from './contract/Greeter.json';

function App() {

  const [greeting, setGreeting] = useState('');

  const [newGreeting, setNewGreeting] = useState('');

  useEffect(() => {

    const loadGreeting = async () => {

      const provider = new ethers.providers.Web3Provider(window.ethereum);

      const contract = new ethers.Contract(Greeter.address, Greeter.abi, provider);

      const greeting = await contract.greet();

      setGreeting(greeting);

    };

    loadGreeting();

  }, []);

  const updateGreeting = async () => {
```

```
    const provider = new
ethers.providers.Web3Provider(window.ethereum);

    const signer = provider.getSigner();

    const contract = new ethers.Contract(Greeter.address,
Greeter.abi, signer);

    const tx = await contract.setGreeting(newGreeting);

    await tx.wait();

    setGreeting(newGreeting);

  };

  return (

   <div>

     <h1>Greeting: {greeting}</h1>

     <input

       type="text"

       value={newGreeting}

       onChange={(e) => setNewGreeting(e.target.value)}

     />

     <button onClick={updateGreeting}>Update Greeting</button>

   </div>

  );

}
```

```
export default App;
```

1.

Deploying to Different Networks

Overview

Deploying smart contracts to different networks involves configuring network settings in Hardhat and using appropriate deployment scripts.

Configuring Networks

Add network configurations to hardhat.config.js:

javascript

Copy code

```javascript
require("@nomiclabs/hardhat-waffle");

module.exports = {
  solidity: "0.8.0",

  networks: {

    ropsten: {

      url:
"https://ropsten.infura.io/v3/YOUR_INFURA_PROJECT_ID",

      accounts: ["YOUR_PRIVATE_KEY"]

    },

    mainnet: {
```

```
    url:
"https://mainnet.infura.io/v3/YOUR_INFURA_PROJECT_ID",

    accounts: ["YOUR_PRIVATE_KEY"]

  }

 }

};
```

Deploying to a Network

To deploy your contract to a specific network, use the following command:

bash

Copy code

```
npx hardhat run scripts/deploy.js --network <network-name>
```

Replace <network-name> with the name of the network you configured, such as ropsten or mainnet.

Summary

In this chapter, we explored advanced Hardhat techniques, including debugging, using plugins, integrating smart contracts with frontend applications, and deploying to different networks. These advanced techniques will help you streamline your development process, optimize gas usage, and create seamless interactions between smart contracts and user interfaces. In the next chapter, we will introduce Foundry, another powerful development tool, and guide you through setting up a Foundry project, compiling and deploying contracts, and writing and running tests.

Chapter 8: Introduction to Foundry

Overview and Installation

What is Foundry?

Foundry is a fast, portable, and modular toolkit for Ethereum application development. It offers a comprehensive suite of tools to compile, deploy, test, and debug smart contracts. Foundry is known for its speed and efficiency, making it a preferred choice for developers seeking high-performance solutions.

Key Features of Foundry

- **High Performance:** Foundry is optimized for speed, enabling quick compilation and testing.
- **Modular Design:** Allows developers to use only the tools they need, making it flexible and lightweight.
- **Scripting:** Supports advanced scripting capabilities for deployment and interaction with contracts.
- **Testing:** Provides robust testing features with advanced capabilities.

Installing Foundry

To install Foundry, follow these steps:

Install Foundryup:
Foundryup is the Foundry toolchain installer and updater.

```
bash
Copy code
curl -L https://foundry.paradigm.xyz | bash
```

1.

Initialize Foundry:
After installing Foundryup, you need to initialize Foundry.
```
bash
Copy code
foundryup
```

1.

Setting Up a Foundry Project

Creating a New Project

To create a new Foundry project, use the following command:

bash

Copy code

```
forge init my-foundry-project

cd my-foundry-project
```

This command will generate a new Foundry project with the following structure:

bash

Copy code

```
my-foundry-project/

├── src/
```

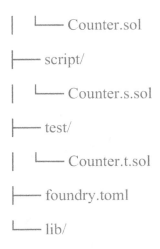

```
|    └── Counter.sol
├── script/
|    └── Counter.s.sol
├── test/
|    └── Counter.t.sol
├── foundry.toml
└── lib/
```

- **src/:** Contains Solidity contract files.

- **script/:** Contains deployment and interaction scripts.

- **test/:** Contains test scripts.

- **foundry.toml:** Configuration file for the project.

- **lib/:** Directory for external libraries.

Configuring Foundry

The foundry.toml file is used to configure your Foundry project. You can specify settings such as compiler version, optimizer settings, and remappings.

toml

Copy code

```
[default]

src = "src"
```

```
out = "out"

libs = ["lib"]

solc_version = "0.8.0"

optimizer = true

optimizer_runs = 200
```

Compiling and Deploying Contracts

Compiling Contracts

To compile your Solidity contracts, run the following command:

bash

Copy code

```
forge build
```

This will compile all the contracts in the src/ directory and generate the necessary artifacts in the out/ directory.

Writing a Deployment Script

Create a deployment script in the script/ directory to deploy your contract.

Create a new file named DeployCounter.s.sol in the script/ directory:
solidity
Copy code
```
// SPDX-License-Identifier: MIT

pragma solidity ^0.8.0;
```

```
import "forge-std/Script.sol";

import "../src/Counter.sol";

contract DeployCounter is Script {

    function run() external {

        vm.startBroadcast();

        Counter counter = new Counter();

        vm.stopBroadcast();

    }

}
```

1.

Run the deployment script:
bash
Copy code
```
forge script script/DeployCounter.s.sol --broadcast --rpc-url <RPC_URL>
```

1. Replace <RPC_URL> with the URL of the network you are deploying to, such as a local node or an Ethereum testnet.

Writing and Running Tests

Writing Tests

Create test scripts in the test/ directory to test your contracts.

Create a new file named CounterTest.t.sol in the test/ directory:

solidity
Copy code

```solidity
// SPDX-License-Identifier: MIT

pragma solidity ^0.8.0;

import "forge-std/Test.sol";

import "../src/Counter.sol";

contract CounterTest is Test {

    Counter counter;

    function setUp() public {

        counter = new Counter();

    }

    function testIncrement() public {

        counter.increment();

        assertEq(counter.getCount(), 1);

    }

    function testDecrement() public {

        counter.increment();

        counter.decrement();

        assertEq(counter.getCount(), 0);

    }

}
```

1.

Running Tests

To run your tests, use the following command:

bash

Copy code

```
forge test
```

This will execute all the test scripts in the test/ directory and display the results.

Summary

In this chapter, we introduced Foundry, a powerful and high-performance toolkit for Ethereum development. We covered the installation process, project setup, and the basic structure of a Foundry project. We also demonstrated how to compile and deploy contracts, and how to write and run tests using Foundry. With these foundational skills, you're well-equipped to develop, test, and deploy Solidity contracts efficiently using Foundry. In the next chapter, we will explore advanced Foundry techniques, including debugging, using plugins, integrating with frontend applications, and deploying to different networks.

Chapter 9: Advanced Foundry Techniques

Debugging with Foundry

Overview

Debugging smart contracts is a critical part of the development process. Foundry provides several tools to help you debug and troubleshoot your contracts effectively.

Foundry Debugger

Foundry includes a powerful debugger that allows you to inspect the state of your contracts and transactions.

Run the Debugger:
To debug a specific transaction, use the forge debug command followed by the transaction hash.
bash
Copy code

```
forge debug <tx-hash>
```

1. Replace <tx-hash> with the actual transaction hash you want to debug.

Using Forge-Std for Logging

Forge-Std is a standard library that includes utilities for logging and debugging.

Install Forge-Std:
bash

Copy code

```
forge install foundry-rs/forge-std
```

1.

Use Logging in Your Contracts:
solidity
Copy code

```solidity
// SPDX-License-Identifier: MIT

pragma solidity ^0.8.0;

import "forge-std/Test.sol";

contract LoggingExample is Test {

    uint256 public value;

    function setValue(uint256 _value) public {

        value = _value;

        emit log_named_uint("Value set to", value);

    }

}
```

1.

Run Tests with Logging:
bash
Copy code

```bash
forge test
```

1. This will output log messages during the test execution, helping you to understand the flow and state changes in your contract.

Using Foundry Plugins

Overview

Foundry supports plugins that extend its functionality. These plugins can help with various tasks such as gas reporting, coverage analysis, and integration with other tools.

Installing and Using Plugins

Install a Plugin:
For example, to install a gas reporter plugin:
bash
Copy code

```
forge install cgewecke/eth-gas-reporter
```

      1.

Configure the Plugin:
Update your foundry.toml to configure the plugin.
toml
Copy code

```
[default]

gas_reports = true
```

      1.

Run Tests with Gas Reporting:
bash
Copy code

```
forge test --gas-reporter
```

      1. This will generate a report showing the gas usage of your contract functions.

Integrating with Frontend Applications

Overview

Integrating smart contracts with frontend applications allows users to interact with the blockchain through a user-friendly interface. We will use React and ethers.js for this purpose.

Setting Up a React Project

Create a new React project:
bash
Copy code

```
npx create-react-app my-dapp

cd my-dapp
```

       1.

Install ethers.js:
bash
Copy code

```
npm install ethers
```

       1.

Connecting to Your Contract

Create a contract directory inside src/ and copy the contract ABI and address:
javascript
Copy code

```
// src/contract/Counter.json

{

  "address": "YOUR_CONTRACT_ADDRESS",

  "abi": [

    // Your contract ABI
```

```
        ]

    }
```

1.

Connect to the contract in your React app:
javascript
Copy code
// src/App.js

```javascript
import React, { useEffect, useState } from 'react';

import { ethers } from 'ethers';

import Counter from './contract/Counter.json';

function App() {

  const [count, setCount] = useState(0);

  const [newCount, setNewCount] = useState(0);

  useEffect(() => {

    const loadCount = async () => {

      const provider = new
ethers.providers.Web3Provider(window.ethereum);

      const contract = new ethers.Contract(Counter.address,
Counter.abi, provider);

      const count = await contract.getCount();

      setCount(count.toNumber());

    };

    loadCount();
```

```
}, []);
const increment = async () => {

  const provider = new
ethers.providers.Web3Provider(window.ethereum);

  const signer = provider.getSigner();

  const contract = new ethers.Contract(Counter.address,
Counter.abi, signer);

  const tx = await contract.increment();

  await tx.wait();

  setCount(count + 1);

};
const decrement = async () => {

  const provider = new
ethers.providers.Web3Provider(window.ethereum);

  const signer = provider.getSigner();

  const contract = new ethers.Contract(Counter.address,
Counter.abi, signer);

  const tx = await contract.decrement();

  await tx.wait();

  setCount(count - 1);

};
return (
```

```
  <div>
    <h1>Count: {count}</h1>
    <button onClick={increment}>Increment</button>
    <button onClick={decrement}>Decrement</button>
  </div>
  );
}
export default App;
```

1.

Deploying to Different Networks

Overview

Deploying smart contracts to different networks involves configuring network settings in Foundry and using appropriate deployment scripts.

Configuring Networks

Add network configurations to your foundry.toml:

toml

Copy code

```
[rpc_endpoints]
mainnet = "https://mainnet.infura.io/v3/YOUR_INFURA_PROJECT_ID"
```

```
ropsten =
"https://ropsten.infura.io/v3/YOUR_INFURA_PROJECT_ID"
```

Deploying to a Network

To deploy your contract to a specific network, use the following command:

bash

Copy code

```
forge script script/DeployCounter.s.sol --broadcast --rpc-url
<RPC_URL>
```

Replace <RPC_URL> with the URL of the network you are deploying to, such as https://ropsten.infura.io/v3/YOUR_INFURA_PROJECT_ID.

Summary

In this chapter, we explored advanced Foundry techniques, including debugging with the Foundry debugger and Forge-Std, using plugins for extended functionality, integrating smart contracts with frontend applications, and deploying to different networks. These advanced techniques will help you streamline your development process, optimize gas usage, and create seamless interactions between smart contracts and user interfaces. In the next chapter, we will discuss how to integrate Hardhat and Foundry in a single project, combining the best features of both tools for efficient and flexible development.

Chapter 10: Integrating Hardhat and Foundry

Overview

Integrating Hardhat and Foundry in a single project allows you to leverage the strengths of both tools, providing a more robust and flexible development environment. This chapter will guide you through the process of setting up a project that uses both Hardhat and Foundry, and demonstrate best practices for development.

Switching Between Hardhat and Foundry

Setting Up the Project

Initialize a Hardhat Project:
bash
Copy code

```
mkdir my-integrated-project

cd my-integrated-project

npx hardhat
```

1. Follow the prompts to create a basic sample project.

Install Foundry:
bash
Copy code

```
curl -L https://foundry.paradigm.xyz | bash

foundryup
```

1.

Create a Foundry Project:
bash
Copy code
```
forge init foundry
```

   1. This creates a foundry/ directory inside your
      Hardhat project.

Project Structure

After setting up both environments, your project structure should
look like this:

bash

Copy code

```
my-integrated-project/
├── contracts/
│   └── Greeter.sol
├── foundry/
│   ├── src/
│   │   └── Counter.sol
│   ├── script/
│   │   └── Counter.s.sol
│   ├── test/
│   │   └── Counter.t.sol
│   └── foundry.toml
├── scripts/
```

```
|     └── deploy.js
├── test/
|     └── greeter-test.js
├── hardhat.config.js
├── package.json
└── node_modules/
```

Configuration Files

Hardhat Configuration (hardhat.config.js):
javascript
Copy code

```javascript
require("@nomiclabs/hardhat-waffle");

module.exports = {
  solidity: "0.8.0",
  networks: {
    hardhat: {},
    ropsten: {
      url:
"https://ropsten.infura.io/v3/YOUR_INFURA_PROJECT_ID",
      accounts: ["YOUR_PRIVATE_KEY"]
    }
  }
};
```

1.

Foundry Configuration (foundry/foundry.toml):
toml
Copy code
```
[default]

src = "src"

out = "out"

libs = ["lib"]

solc_version = "0.8.0"

optimizer = true

optimizer_runs = 200
```

1.

Combining Hardhat and Foundry in a Single Project

Compilation

You can compile your contracts using both Hardhat and Foundry:

Compile with Hardhat:
bash
Copy code
```
npx hardhat compile
```

1.

Compile with Foundry:
bash

Copy code
```
cd foundry

forge build
```

1.

Deployment

Deploy contracts using Hardhat and Foundry deployment scripts.

Deploy with Hardhat:
javascript
Copy code
```javascript
// scripts/deploy.js

async function main() {

  const [deployer] = await ethers.getSigners();

  console.log("Deploying contracts with the account:",
deployer.address);

  const Greeter = await ethers.getContractFactory("Greeter");

  const greeter = await Greeter.deploy("Hello, Hardhat!");

  console.log("Greeter deployed to:", greeter.address);

}

main()

  .then(() => process.exit(0))

  .catch((error) => {

    console.error(error);

    process.exit(1);
```

```
});
```

Run the deployment script:
bash
Copy code
```
npx hardhat run scripts/deploy.js --network ropsten
```

1.

Deploy with Foundry:
solidity
Copy code
```solidity
// foundry/script/DeployCounter.s.sol

// SPDX-License-Identifier: MIT

pragma solidity ^0.8.0;

import "forge-std/Script.sol";

import "../src/Counter.sol";

contract DeployCounter is Script {

    function run() external {

        vm.startBroadcast();

        Counter counter = new Counter();

        vm.stopBroadcast();

    }

}
```

Run the deployment script:
bash
Copy code

```
forge script script/DeployCounter.s.sol --broadcast --rpc-url
<RPC_URL>
```

1.

Testing

Write and run tests using both Hardhat and Foundry testing
frameworks.

Test with Hardhat:
javascript
Copy code
```javascript
// test/greeter-test.js

const { expect } = require("chai");

describe("Greeter", function () {

  it("Should return the new greeting once it's changed", async
function () {

    const Greeter = await ethers.getContractFactory("Greeter");

    const greeter = await Greeter.deploy("Hello, world!");

    await greeter.deployed();

    expect(await greeter.greet()).to.equal("Hello, world!");

    const setGreetingTx = await greeter.setGreeting("Hola,
mundo!");

    // wait until the transaction is mined

    await setGreetingTx.wait();

    expect(await greeter.greet()).to.equal("Hola, mundo!");
```

```
});

});
```

Run the tests:
bash
Copy code
```
npx hardhat test
```

1.

Test with Foundry:
solidity
Copy code
```
// foundry/test/CounterTest.t.sol

// SPDX-License-Identifier: MIT

pragma solidity ^0.8.0;

import "forge-std/Test.sol";

import "../src/Counter.sol";

contract CounterTest is Test {

    Counter counter;

    function setUp() public {

        counter = new Counter();

    }

    function testIncrement() public {

        counter.increment();

        assertEq(counter.getCount(), 1);
```

```
    }

    function testDecrement() public {

        counter.increment();

        counter.decrement();

        assertEq(counter.getCount(), 0);

    }

}
```

Run the tests:
bash
Copy code
```
forge test
```

       1.

Best Practices for Development

Code Consistency

Maintain a consistent coding style across Hardhat and Foundry to ensure readability and maintainability. Use tools like Prettier and Solhint for linting and formatting.

Modular Design

Keep your contract logic modular by separating concerns into different contracts and libraries. This practice enhances code reusability and simplifies testing and maintenance.

Continuous Integration

Integrate Hardhat and Foundry tests into your continuous integration (CI) pipeline to automate testing and deployment. Use services like GitHub Actions, CircleCI, or Travis CI to run your tests on every code push.

Documentation

Document your code thoroughly using NatSpec comments and maintain updated README files for your project. Good documentation helps other developers understand and contribute to your project effectively.

Summary

In this chapter, we explored how to integrate Hardhat and Foundry in a single project to leverage the strengths of both tools. We covered setting up the project, configuring both environments, compiling, deploying, and testing contracts, and best practices for development. By combining Hardhat and Foundry, you can create a robust and flexible development environment that maximizes productivity and code quality. In the next chapter, we will delve into real-world applications and projects, demonstrating how to build a decentralized exchange, create an NFT marketplace, and develop a DAO.

Chapter 11: Real-World Applications and Projects

Building a Decentralized Exchange (DEX)

Overview

A Decentralized Exchange (DEX) is a type of cryptocurrency exchange that operates without a central authority. It allows users to trade cryptocurrencies directly with each other using smart contracts. In this section, we'll build a simple DEX that supports token swaps.

Designing the DEX

1. **Token Contract:** We'll use an ERC20 token standard for the tokens being traded on the DEX.
2. **DEX Contract:** The DEX contract will handle the swapping logic between two ERC20 tokens.

Token Contract

ERC20 Token Contract:
solidity
Copy code

```
// SPDX-License-Identifier: MIT

pragma solidity ^0.8.0;

import "@openzeppelin/contracts/token/ERC20/ERC20.sol";

contract Token is ERC20 {
```

```
constructor(string memory name, string memory symbol,
uint256 initialSupply) ERC20(name, symbol) {

    _mint(msg.sender, initialSupply);

}

}
```

1.

Deploying the Token Contract:
javascript
Copy code
```javascript
async function main() {

    const [deployer] = await ethers.getSigners();

    console.log("Deploying contracts with the account:",
deployer.address);

    const Token = await ethers.getContractFactory("Token");

    const tokenA = await Token.deploy("TokenA", "TKA",
ethers.utils.parseUnits("1000000", 18));

    const tokenB = await Token.deploy("TokenB", "TKB",
ethers.utils.parseUnits("1000000", 18));

    console.log("TokenA deployed to:", tokenA.address);

    console.log("TokenB deployed to:", tokenB.address);

}

main()

  .then(() => process.exit(0))

  .catch(error => {
```

```
    console.error(error);

    process.exit(1);

  });
```

1.

DEX Contract

DEX Contract:
solidity
Copy code

```solidity
// SPDX-License-Identifier: MIT

pragma solidity ^0.8.0;

import "@openzeppelin/contracts/token/ERC20/IERC20.sol";

import "@openzeppelin/contracts/security/ReentrancyGuard.sol";

contract SimpleDEX is ReentrancyGuard {

    IERC20 public tokenA;

    IERC20 public tokenB;

    uint256 public rate; // Exchange rate: 1 TokenA = rate TokenB

    constructor(IERC20 _tokenA, IERC20 _tokenB, uint256 _rate) {

        tokenA = _tokenA;

        tokenB = _tokenB;

        rate = _rate;

    }
```

```solidity
function swapAToB(uint256 _amountA) public nonReentrant {

    require(tokenA.transferFrom(msg.sender, address(this),
_amountA), "Transfer of TokenA failed");

    uint256 amountB = _amountA * rate;

    require(tokenB.transfer(msg.sender, amountB), "Transfer of
TokenB failed");

    }

    function swapBToA(uint256 _amountB) public nonReentrant {

    require(tokenB.transferFrom(msg.sender, address(this),
_amountB), "Transfer of TokenB failed");

    uint256 amountA = _amountB / rate;

    require(tokenA.transfer(msg.sender, amountA), "Transfer of
TokenA failed");

    }

}
```

1.

Deploying the DEX Contract:
javascript
Copy code
```javascript
async function main() {

    const [deployer] = await ethers.getSigners();

    console.log("Deploying contracts with the account:",
deployer.address);

    const Token = await ethers.getContractFactory("Token");
```

```javascript
    const tokenA = await Token.deploy("TokenA", "TKA",
ethers.utils.parseUnits("1000000", 18));

    const tokenB = await Token.deploy("TokenB", "TKB",
ethers.utils.parseUnits("1000000", 18));

    await tokenA.deployed();

    await tokenB.deployed();

    const SimpleDEX = await
ethers.getContractFactory("SimpleDEX");

    const dex = await SimpleDEX.deploy(tokenA.address,
tokenB.address, 100); // 1 TKA = 100 TKB

    console.log("SimpleDEX deployed to:", dex.address);

}

main()

  .then(() => process.exit(0))

  .catch(error => {

    console.error(error);

    process.exit(1);

  });
```

1.

Creating an NFT Marketplace

Overview

A Non-Fungible Token (NFT) Marketplace is a platform where users can buy, sell, and trade unique digital assets represented as NFTs. In this section, we'll build a simple NFT marketplace that allows users to list and buy NFTs.

Designing the NFT Marketplace

1. **NFT Contract:** We'll use the ERC721 token standard for NFTs.
2. **Marketplace Contract:** The marketplace contract will handle listing NFTs for sale and buying listed NFTs.

NFT Contract

ERC721 NFT Contract:
solidity
Copy code

```solidity
// SPDX-License-Identifier: MIT

pragma solidity ^0.8.0;

import "@openzeppelin/contracts/token/ERC721/ERC721.sol";

import "@openzeppelin/contracts/access/Ownable.sol";

contract NFT is ERC721, Ownable {

    uint256 public tokenCounter;

    constructor() ERC721("MyNFT", "NFT") {

        tokenCounter = 0;

    }

    function createNFT() public onlyOwner returns (uint256) {

        uint256 newTokenId = tokenCounter;
```

```
    _safeMint(msg.sender, newTokenId);

    tokenCounter += 1;

    return newTokenId;

  }

}
```

1.

Deploying the NFT Contract:
javascript
Copy code

```javascript
async function main() {

  const [deployer] = await ethers.getSigners();

  console.log("Deploying contracts with the account:",
deployer.address);

  const NFT = await ethers.getContractFactory("NFT");

  const nft = await NFT.deploy();

  console.log("NFT deployed to:", nft.address);

}

main()

 .then(() => process.exit(0))

 .catch(error => {

  console.error(error);

  process.exit(1);
```

```
});
```

1.

Marketplace Contract

Marketplace Contract:
solidity
Copy code
// SPDX-License-Identifier: MIT

pragma solidity ^0.8.0;

import "@openzeppelin/contracts/token/ERC721/IERC721.sol";

import "@openzeppelin/contracts/security/ReentrancyGuard.sol";

contract NFTMarketplace is ReentrancyGuard {

    struct Listing {

        uint256 price;

        address seller;

    }

    IERC721 public nftContract;

    mapping(uint256 => Listing) public listings;

    constructor(IERC721 _nftContract) {

        nftContract = _nftContract;

    }

    function listNFT(uint256 _tokenId, uint256 _price) public {

```solidity
        require(nftContract.ownerOf(_tokenId) == msg.sender, "Not
the owner");

        require(_price > 0, "Price must be greater than zero");

        nftContract.transferFrom(msg.sender, address(this),
_tokenId);

        listings[_tokenId] = Listing(_price, msg.sender);

    }

    function buyNFT(uint256 _tokenId) public payable
nonReentrant {

        Listing memory listing = listings[_tokenId];

        require(msg.value >= listing.price, "Insufficient payment");

        delete listings[_tokenId];

        nftContract.transferFrom(address(this), msg.sender,
_tokenId);

        payable(listing.seller).transfer(msg.value);

    }

}
```

1.

Deploying the Marketplace Contract:
javascript
Copy code

```javascript
async function main() {

    const [deployer] = await ethers.getSigners();
```

```
  console.log("Deploying contracts with the account:",
deployer.address);

  const NFT = await ethers.getContractFactory("NFT");

  const nft = await NFT.deploy();

  await nft.deployed();

  const NFTMarketplace = await
ethers.getContractFactory("NFTMarketplace");

  const marketplace = await
NFTMarketplace.deploy(nft.address);

  console.log("NFTMarketplace deployed to:",
marketplace.address);

}

main()

  .then(() => process.exit(0))

  .catch(error => {

  console.error(error);

  process.exit(1);

  });
```

1.

Developing a DAO

Overview

A Decentralized Autonomous Organization (DAO) is an organization governed by smart contracts and community voting. In this section, we'll build a simple DAO that allows members to create and vote on proposals.

Designing the DAO

1. **Governance Token:** We'll use an ERC20 token as the governance token for the DAO.
2. **DAO Contract:** The DAO contract will handle creating and voting on proposals.

Governance Token

ERC20 Governance Token:
solidity
Copy code
```solidity
// SPDX-License-Identifier: MIT

pragma solidity ^0.8.0;

import "@openzeppelin/contracts/token/ERC20/ERC20.sol";

contract GovernanceToken is ERC20 {

    constructor(uint256 initialSupply) ERC20("GovernanceToken", "GT") {

        _mint(msg.sender, initialSupply);

    }

}
```

1.

Deploying the Governance Token:
javascript

Copy code

```
async function main() {

    const [deployer] = await ethers.getSigners();

    console.log("Deploying contracts with the account:",
deployer.address);

    const GovernanceToken = await
ethers.getContractFactory("GovernanceToken");

    const token = await
GovernanceToken.deploy(ethers.utils.parseUnits("1000000", 18));

    console.log("GovernanceToken deployed to:", token.address);

}

main()

  .then(() => process.exit(0))

  .catch(error => {

    console.error(error);

    process.exit(1);

  });
```

1.

DAO Contract

DAO Contract:
solidity
Copy code
// SPDX-License-Identifier: MIT

```solidity
pragma solidity ^0.8.0;

import "@openzeppelin/contracts/token/ERC20/IERC20.sol";

contract DAO {

    struct Proposal {

        string description;

        uint256 votesFor;

        uint256 votesAgainst;

        uint256 deadline;

        bool executed;

        mapping(address => bool) voters;

    }

    IERC20 public governanceToken;

    uint256 public proposalCount;

    mapping(uint256 => Proposal) public proposals;

    constructor(IERC20 _governanceToken) {

        governanceToken = _governanceToken;

    }

    function createProposal(string memory _description) public {

        proposalCount++;

        Proposal storage proposal = proposals[proposalCount];
```

```solidity
        proposal.description = _description;

        proposal.deadline = block.timestamp + 1 weeks;

    }

    function vote(uint256 _proposalId, bool _support) public {

        Proposal storage proposal = proposals[_proposalId];

        require(block.timestamp < proposal.deadline, "Voting period
ended");

        require(!proposal.voters[msg.sender], "Already voted");

        uint256 balance = governanceToken.balanceOf(msg.sender);

        require(balance > 0, "No governance tokens");

        proposal.voters[msg.sender] = true;

        if (_support) {

            proposal.votesFor += balance;

        } else {

            proposal.votesAgainst += balance;

        }

    }

    function executeProposal(uint256 _proposalId) public {

        Proposal storage proposal = proposals[_proposalId];

        require(block.timestamp >= proposal.deadline, "Voting
period not ended");
```

```
require(!proposal.executed, "Proposal already executed");

proposal.executed = true;

// Implement proposal execution logic

}

}
```

1.

Deploying the DAO Contract:
javascript
Copy code

```javascript
async function main() {

    const [deployer] = await ethers.getSigners();

    console.log("Deploying contracts with the account:",
deployer.address);

    const GovernanceToken = await
ethers.getContractFactory("GovernanceToken");

    const token = await
GovernanceToken.deploy(ethers.utils.parseUnits("1000000", 18));

    await token.deployed();

    const DAO = await ethers.getContractFactory("DAO");

    const dao = await DAO.deploy(token.address);

    console.log("DAO deployed to:", dao.address);

}

main()
```

```
.then(() => process.exit(0))

.catch(error => {

  console.error(error);

  process.exit(1);

});
```

1.

Case Studies and Examples

Case Study: Uniswap

Uniswap is a popular decentralized exchange that allows users to trade ERC20 tokens directly from their wallets. It uses an automated market maker (AMM) model to facilitate trades and provide liquidity.

Case Study: OpenSea

OpenSea is a leading NFT marketplace that allows users to buy, sell, and trade NFTs. It supports a wide range of digital assets, including art, collectibles, and virtual real estate.

Case Study: MakerDAO

MakerDAO is a decentralized autonomous organization that manages the DAI stablecoin. It uses smart contracts to maintain the stability of DAI and allows users to generate DAI by locking up collateral in the form of ETH or other ERC20 tokens.

Summary

In this chapter, we explored the development of real-world applications and projects, including a decentralized exchange (DEX), an NFT marketplace, and a DAO. We covered the design and implementation of these projects using Solidity and provided deployment scripts to launch them on the Ethereum network. We also discussed case studies of popular decentralized applications (dApps) to provide insights into their architecture and functionality. In the next chapter, we will discuss best practices and tips for Solidity development, including code style, documentation, performance optimization, and community resources for further learning.

Chapter 12: Best Practices and Tips

Code Style and Documentation

Code Style

Adhering to a consistent code style is crucial for maintaining readability and maintainability in your Solidity projects. Here are some best practices:

1. **Formatting:**
   - Use indentation to enhance readability. The standard is 4 spaces.
   - Break long lines at a reasonable length (e.g., 80-120 characters).

solidity
Copy code
```
// Good

uint256 public totalSupply = 1000000;

// Bad

uint256 public totalSupply=1000000;
```

1.
2. **Naming Conventions:**
   - Use camelCase for variables and function names.
   -

Use PascalCase for contract names.

○

Use ALL_CAPS for constants.

solidity
Copy code
```
// Good

uint256 public totalSupply;

function getBalance() public view returns (uint256);

// Bad

uint256 public Total_Supply;

function get_balance() public view returns (uint256);
```

1.
2. **Comments:**
   ○
   Use comments to explain complex logic and provide context.
   ○

   Use NatSpec comments for functions and contracts.

solidity
Copy code
```
/**

* @dev Transfers tokens to a specified address.

* @param to The address to transfer to.

* @param value The amount to be transferred.

*/
```

```solidity
function transfer(address to, uint256 value) public returns (bool) {

    // Ensure the sender has enough balance

    require(balanceOf[msg.sender] >= value, "Insufficient balance");

    // Transfer the value

    balanceOf[msg.sender] -= value;

    balanceOf[to] += value;

    return true;

}
```

1.

Documentation

Proper documentation is essential for understanding and maintaining your codebase. Here are some tips:

1. **NatSpec Documentation:**
   -

   Use NatSpec for documenting functions, parameters, return values, and events.

solidity
Copy code
```
/**

* @title SimpleStorage

* @dev Store & retrieve value in a variable

*/
```

```
contract SimpleStorage {

    uint256 public storedData;

    /**

     * @dev Store value in variable

     * @param x value to store

     */

    function set(uint256 x) public {

        storedData = x;

    }

    /**

     * @dev Return value

     * @return value of 'storedData'

     */

    function get() public view returns (uint256) {

        return storedData;

    }

}
```

1.
2. **README Files:**
   ○

Include a README file in your project to provide an overview, installation instructions, usage examples, and contribution guidelines.

markdown
Copy code
SimpleStorage

SimpleStorage is a smart contract for storing and retrieving a value.

Installation

1. Clone the repository

2. Install dependencies: `npm install`

3. Compile the contracts: `npx hardhat compile`

Usage

Deploy the contract:

```bash

npx hardhat run scripts/deploy.js --network ropsten
```

Interact with the contract:
javascript
Copy code
```javascript
const SimpleStorage = await
ethers.getContractFactory("SimpleStorage");

const simpleStorage = await SimpleStorage.deploy();

await simpleStorage.set(42);

console.log(await simpleStorage.get());
```

1. # Contributing

Contributions are welcome! Please submit a pull request or open an issue.
Copy code

Performance Optimization

Gas Optimization

Gas optimization is essential for reducing transaction costs and making your smart contracts more efficient. Here are some tips:

1. **Minimize Storage Writes:**
   o

   Writing to storage is expensive. Minimize the number of storage writes in your contract.

solidity
Copy code

```
// Inefficient

function increment() public {

  count = count + 1;

}

// Efficient

function increment() public {

  uint256 newCount = count + 1;

  count = newCount;

}
```

1.
2. **Use calldata for Function Parameters:**
   ○

   When possible, use calldata instead of memory for function parameters.

solidity
Copy code
```
// More expensive

function processData(string memory data) public {

    // ...

}

// Less expensive

function processData(string calldata data) public {

    // ...

}
```

1.
2. **Avoid Dynamic Arrays in Storage:**
   ○

   Dynamic arrays in storage are expensive to manage. Use fixed-size arrays or mappings when possible.

solidity
Copy code
```
// Inefficient

uint256[] public dynamicArray;

// Efficient
```

112

```solidity
uint256[10] public fixedArray;
```

1.

Optimizer Settings

Use the Solidity optimizer to reduce gas costs. Configure the optimizer in your Hardhat or Foundry project:

Hardhat (hardhat.config.js):

javascript

Copy code

```javascript
module.exports = {
  solidity: {
    version: "0.8.0",
    settings: {
      optimizer: {
        enabled: true,
        runs: 200,
      },
    },
  },
};
```

Foundry (foundry.toml):

toml

Copy code

```
[default]

solc_version = "0.8.0"

optimizer = true

optimizer_runs = 200
```

Community Resources and Further Learning

Community Resources

1. **Solidity Documentation:**
   - The official Solidity documentation is a comprehensive resource for learning Solidity: Solidity Docs
1. **Ethereum Stack Exchange:**
   - A Q&A site for Ethereum developers: Ethereum Stack Exchange
1. **Ethereum Developer Portal:**
   - Resources and guides for Ethereum development: Ethereum Developer Portal
1. **OpenZeppelin:**
   - Secure smart contract libraries and tools: OpenZeppelin

Further Learning

1. **Courses and Tutorials:**

o

CryptoZombies: An interactive Solidity tutorial.

o

Consensys Academy: Ethereum developer courses.

1. **Books:**

    o

    "Mastering Ethereum" by Andreas M. Antonopoulos and Gavin Wood: A comprehensive guide to Ethereum development.

    o

    "Building Ethereum Dapps" by Roberto Infante: A practical guide to developing decentralized applications on Ethereum.

1. **Conferences and Meetups:**

    o

    Attend blockchain and Ethereum conferences, such as Devcon, EthCC, and local Ethereum meetups, to network with other developers and learn about the latest advancements.

Summary

In this chapter, we discussed best practices and tips for Solidity development, including code style, documentation, performance optimization, and community resources for further learning. Adhering to these best practices will help you write clean, efficient, and secure smart contracts. As you continue your journey in blockchain development, staying engaged with the community and continually learning will be crucial for your success. In the next chapter, we will provide appendices with a glossary of terms, useful tools and resources, and references for further reading.

Chapter 13: Appendices

Glossary of Terms

General Blockchain Terms

- **Blockchain:** A decentralized and distributed digital ledger that records transactions across many computers in a way that ensures the security and immutability of the data.
- **Decentralization:** The distribution of authority, control, and function away from a central authority or location.
- **Node:** A computer connected to the blockchain network that validates and relays transactions.
- **Consensus Mechanism:** A method used by blockchain networks to achieve agreement on the state of the ledger. Examples include Proof of Work (PoW) and Proof of Stake (PoS).
- **Smart Contract:** Self-executing contracts with the terms of the agreement directly written into code and stored on the blockchain.

- **Gas:** A unit that measures the amount of computational effort required to execute operations on the Ethereum network.

Solidity Terms

-

Solidity: A statically-typed programming language designed for developing smart contracts on the Ethereum Virtual Machine (EVM).

- **EVM (Ethereum Virtual Machine):** A Turing-complete virtual machine that executes smart contracts on the Ethereum network.

- **ABI (Application Binary Interface):** A standard for interacting with smart contracts, defining how to encode/decode data and interact with contract functions.

- **ERC20:** A standard interface for fungible tokens on the Ethereum blockchain.

- **ERC721:** A standard interface for non-fungible tokens (NFTs) on the Ethereum blockchain.

- **Modifier:** A keyword used in Solidity to change the behavior of a function or to add conditions to its execution.

Development Tools

- **Hardhat:** A development environment for compiling, deploying, testing, and debugging Ethereum smart contracts.

- **Foundry:** A high-performance toolkit for Ethereum development, offering fast compilation, testing, and deployment.

- **Remix:** An online IDE for writing, testing, and deploying Solidity smart contracts.

-

Truffle: A development framework for Ethereum that provides tools for smart contract compilation, deployment, and testing.

-

Ganache: A personal blockchain for Ethereum development, allowing developers to deploy and test contracts locally.

Useful Tools and Resources

Development Tools

1. **Hardhat:**
   - Website:Hardhat
   - Documentation: Hardhat Docs
1. **Foundry:**
   - GitHub:Foundry GitHub
   - Documentation: Foundry Docs
1. **Remix IDE:**
   - Website: Remix IDE
   - Documentation:Remix Docs
1. **Truffle Suite:**
   - Website:Truffle
   - Documentation: Truffle Docs
1. **Ganache:**
   - Website: Ganache
   -

Documentation: Ganache Docs

Libraries and Frameworks

1. **OpenZeppelin:**
   - Website:OpenZeppelin
   - Documentation: OpenZeppelin Docs
1. **Ethers.js:**
   - GitHub:Ethers.js GitHub
   - Documentation: Ethers.js Docs
1. **Web3.js:**
   - GitHub:Web3.js GitHub
   -

   Documentation:Web3.js Docs

Security Tools

1. **MythX:**
   - Website:MythX
   - Documentation: MythX Docs
1. **Slither:**
   - GitHub:Slither GitHub
   - Documentation:Slither Docs
1. **Echidna:**
   - GitHub:Echidna GitHub
   -

Documentation:Echidna Docs

Learning Resources

1. **CryptoZombies:**
   - Website:CryptoZombies
   - Description: An interactive tutorial that teaches you Solidity by building a zombie game.
1. **Consensys Academy:**
   - Website: Consensys Academy
   - Description: Offers comprehensive Ethereum developer courses.
1. **Ethereum.org Developer Portal:**
   - Website: Ethereum.org Developers
   - Description: Provides a wide range of resources and guides for Ethereum development.

References and Further Reading

1. **Mastering Ethereum by Andreas M. Antonopoulos and Gavin Wood:**
   - A comprehensive guide to understanding and developing on the Ethereum platform.
1. **Building Ethereum Dapps by Roberto Infante:**
   - A practical guide to building decentralized applications on the Ethereum blockchain.
1. **Ethereum Whitepaper:**
   -

Website: Ethereum Whitepaper

o

Description: The original whitepaper by Vitalik Buterin outlining the Ethereum protocol and vision.

1. **Solidity Documentation:**

   o

   Website: Solidity Docs

   o

   Description: Official documentation for the Solidity programming language.

1. **Ethereum Yellow Paper:**

   o

   Website: Ethereum Yellow Paper

   o

   Description: A technical definition of the Ethereum protocol by Dr. Gavin Wood.

Summary

In this chapter, we provided a glossary of key terms, a list of useful tools and resources, and references for further reading. These resources are essential for deepening your understanding of blockchain and smart contract development and for staying up-to-date with the latest advancements in the field. As you continue your journey, leveraging these tools and resources will help you build robust and innovative decentralized applications. In the final chapter, we will recap the key points covered in this book, provide some final thoughts and encouragement, and discuss the next steps in your development journey.

Chapter 14: Conclusion

Recap and Next Steps

Recap of Key Points

Throughout this book, we have covered a comprehensive range of topics essential for mastering Solidity programming and Ethereum development. Let's recap the key points from each chapter:

1. **Introduction to Solidity Programming:**
   - We introduced blockchain and smart contracts, explained the importance of Solidity, and set up the development environment using Hardhat and Foundry.
1. **Solidity Basics:**
   - Covered fundamental concepts such as data types, variables, functions, conditionals, arrays, structs, mappings, enums, and control structures.
1. **Contract Development:**
   - Walked through creating and deploying your first contract, inheritance and visibility, function modifiers, and events and logging.
1. **Advanced Solidity Concepts:**
   - Discussed error handling, gas optimization techniques, inline assembly, and proxy contracts for upgrades.
1. **Smart Contract Security:**
   -

Explored common vulnerabilities, best practices for secure coding, and methods for auditing and testing your contracts.

1. **Introduction to Hardhat:**
   o

   Provided an overview of Hardhat, project setup, compiling and deploying contracts, and writing and running tests.

1. **Advanced Hardhat Techniques:**
   o

   Covered debugging, using plugins, integrating with frontend applications, and deploying to different networks.

1. **Introduction to Foundry:**
   o

   Introduced Foundry, project setup, compiling and deploying contracts, and writing and running tests.

1. **Advanced Foundry Techniques:**
   o

   Discussed debugging, using plugins, integrating with frontend applications, and deploying to different networks.

1. **Integrating Hardhat and Foundry:**
   o

   Explained how to combine Hardhat and Foundry in a single project, ensuring seamless development and testing.

1. **Real-World Applications and Projects:**
   o

   Provided practical examples of building a decentralized exchange (DEX), an NFT marketplace, and a DAO, along with case studies.

1. **Best Practices and Tips:**
   o

   Shared insights on code style, documentation, performance optimization, and community resources for further learning.

1. **Appendices:**
   o

   Offered a glossary of terms, useful tools and resources, and references for further reading.

Next Steps

Now that you have a solid foundation in Solidity programming and Ethereum development, here are some next steps to further your journey:

1. **Build and Deploy Your Projects:**
   o

   Apply the concepts learned in this book to build and deploy your own smart contracts and decentralized applications.
1. **Contribute to Open Source Projects:**
   o

   Join and contribute to open source blockchain projects on platforms like GitHub to gain practical experience and collaborate with other developers.
1. **Stay Updated:**
   o

   Keep up with the latest advancements in the Ethereum ecosystem by following blogs, attending conferences, and participating in community discussions.
1. **Explore Advanced Topics:**
   o

   Delve deeper into advanced topics such as layer 2 solutions, cross-chain interoperability, zero-knowledge proofs, and decentralized finance (DeFi).
1. **Security Audits:**
   o

Learn more about conducting thorough security audits and consider getting your projects audited by professional firms to ensure their robustness.

Final Thoughts and Encouragement

Embarking on the journey of blockchain and smart contract development can be both challenging and rewarding. As you continue to hone your skills, remember these key points:

- **Stay Curious:** The blockchain space is constantly evolving. Stay curious and open to learning new concepts and technologies.
- **Collaborate:** Engage with the community, share your knowledge, and learn from others. Collaboration often leads to innovative solutions and opportunities.
- **Focus on Security:** Security is paramount in blockchain development. Always prioritize secure coding practices and remain vigilant against potential vulnerabilities.
- **Experiment:** Don't be afraid to experiment with new ideas and projects. The best way to learn is by doing and iterating on your work.

- **Be Patient:** Mastery takes time. Be patient with your learning process and celebrate your progress along the way.

Encouragement

Your journey in blockchain development is just beginning, and the potential for innovation is limitless. By mastering Solidity and Ethereum development, you are equipped to create decentralized applications that can revolutionize industries and empower individuals. Stay passionate, keep building, and continue pushing the boundaries of what is possible.

Thank you for taking this journey with us. We wish you all the best in your future endeavors and look forward to seeing the incredible contributions you will make to the blockchain ecosystem.

Happy coding!

Summary

In this concluding chapter, we recapped the key points covered in the book, provided next steps to further your journey, and offered final thoughts and encouragement. As you move forward, remember to stay curious, collaborate with others, prioritize security, experiment with new ideas, and be patient with your progress. Your efforts in mastering Solidity and Ethereum development will pave the way for creating impactful decentralized applications and driving innovation in the blockchain space.

www.ingramcontent.com/pod-product-compliance
Lightning Source LLC
LaVergne TN
LVHW051659050326
832903LV00032B/3903